TIM ALLEN

OVERCOMING ADVERSITY

TIM ALLEN

John Wukovits

Chelsea House Publishers
Philadelphia

Frontis: Tim Allen overcame troubles with the law when he was young to build a successful career as one of America's most popular comedians and entertainers.

CHELSEA HOUSE PUBLISHERS

EDITOR IN CHIEF Stephen Reginald
PRODUCTION MANAGER Pamela Loos
MANAGING EDITOR James D. Gallagher
PICTURE EDITOR Judy L. Hasday
ART DIRECTOR Sara Davis
SENIOR PRODUCTION EDITOR Lisa Chippendale

Staff for **Tim Allen**
ASSOCIATE ART DIRECTOR Takeshi Takahashi
DESIGNER Terry Mallon
PICTURE RESEARCHER Sandy Jones
COVER DESIGN Keith Trego
COVER ILLUSTRATION Rip Kastaris

First Printing

1 3 5 7 9 8 6 4 2

Library of Congress Cataloging-in-Publication Data

Wukovits, John F., 1944-
Tim Allen / John Wukovits.
112 p.   cm. — (Overcoming Adversity)
Includes bibliographical references and index.
Summary: Presents a biography of the star of the television show "Home Improvement," focusing on how he turned his life around after serving a prison sentence for selling illegal drugs.

ISBN 0-7910-4696-6 (hardcover).—ISBN 0-7910-4697-4 (pbk.)
1. Allen, Tim, 1953- —Juvenile literature. 2. Television actors and actress-es—United States—Biography—Juvenile literature. 3. Comedians—United States—Biography—Juvenile literature. 4. Allen, Tim, 1953-. [1. Actors and actresses. 2. Comedians.]
I. Title.   II. Series.
PN2287.A488W85   1998
791.45'028'092—dc21
[B]   98-13039
                                                                          CIP
                                                                          AC

CONTENTS

OVERCOMING ADVERSITY

TIM ALLEN
comedian/performer

JIM CARREY
comedian/performer

BILL CLINTON
U.S. President

JAMES EARL JONES
actor

ABRAHAM LINCOLN
U.S. President

WILLIAM PENN
Pennsylvania's founder

ROSEANNE
entertainer

INTRODUCTION

James Scott Brady

I GUESS IT'S a long way from a Centralia, Illinois, train yard to the George Washington University Hospital Trauma Unit. My dad was a yardmaster for the old Chicago, Burlington & Quincy Railroad. As a child, I used to get to sit in the engineer's lap and imagine what it was like to drive that train. I guess I always have liked being in the "driver's seat."

Years later, however, my interest turned from driving trains to driving campaigns. In 1979, former Texas governor John Connally hired me as a press secretary in his campaign for the American presidency. We lost the Republican primary to a former Hollywood star named Ronald Reagan. But I managed to jump over to the Reagan campaign. When Reagan was elected in 1980, I was "sitting in the catbird seat," as humorist James Thurber would say—poised to be named presidential press secretary. I held that title throughout the eight years of the Reagan administration. But not without one terrible, extended interruption.

It happened barely two months after the Reagan administration took office. I never even heard the shots. On March 30, 1981, my life went blank in an instant. In an attempt to assassinate President Reagan, John Hinckley Jr. armed himself with a "Saturday night special"—a low-quality, $29 pistol—and shot wildly as our presidential entourage exited a Washington hotel. One of the exploding bullets struck me just above the left eye. It shattered into a couple dozen fragments, some of which penetrated my skull and entered my brain.

The next few months of my life were a nightmare of repeated surgery, broken contact with the outside world, and a variety of medical complications. More than once, I was very close to death.

The next few years were filled with frustrating struggles to function with a paralyzed right side, struggles to speak and communicate.

To people who face and defeat daunting obstacles, "ambition" is not becoming wealthy or famous or winning elections or awards. Words like "ambition" and "achievement" and "success" take on very different meanings. The objective is just to live, to wake up every morning. The goals are not lofty; they are very ordinary.

My own heroes are ordinary folks—but they accomplish extraordinary things because they try. My greatest hero is my wife, Sarah. She's accomplished a lot of things in life, but two stand out. The first has been the way she has cared for me and our son since I was shot. A tremendous tragedy and burden was dropped unexpectedly into her life, totally beyond her control and without justification. She could have given up; instead, she focused her energies on preserving our family and returning our lives to normal as much as possible. Week by week, month by month, year by year, she has not reached for the miraculous, just for the normal. Yet in focusing on the normal, she has helped accomplish the miraculous.

Her other most remarkable accomplishment, to me, has been spearheading the effort to keep guns out of the hands of criminals and children in America. Opponents call her a "gun grabber"; I call her a national hero. And I am not alone.

After a seven-year battle, during which Sarah and I worked tirelessly to educate the public about the need for stronger gun laws, the Brady Bill became law in 1993. It was a victory, achieved in the face of tremendous opposition, that now benefits all Americans. From the time the law took effect through fall 1997, background checks had stopped 173,000 criminals and other high-risk purchasers from buying handguns, and the law has helped to reduce illegal gun trafficking.

Sarah was not pursuing fame, or even recognition. She simply started at one point—when our son, Scott, found a loaded handgun on the seat of a pickup truck and, thinking it was a toy, pointed it at Sarah.

Fortunately, no one was hurt. But seeing a gun nearly bring a second tragedy upon our family, Sarah became determined to do whatever she could to prevent senseless death and injury from guns.

Some people think of Sarah as a powerful political force. To me, she's the person who so many times fed me and helped me dress during my long years of recovery.

Overcoming obstacles is part of life, not just for people who are challenged by disabilities, illnesses, or tragedies, but for all people. No matter what the obstacle—fear, disability, prejudice, grief, or a difficulty that isn't likely to "just go away"—we can all work to make this world a better place.

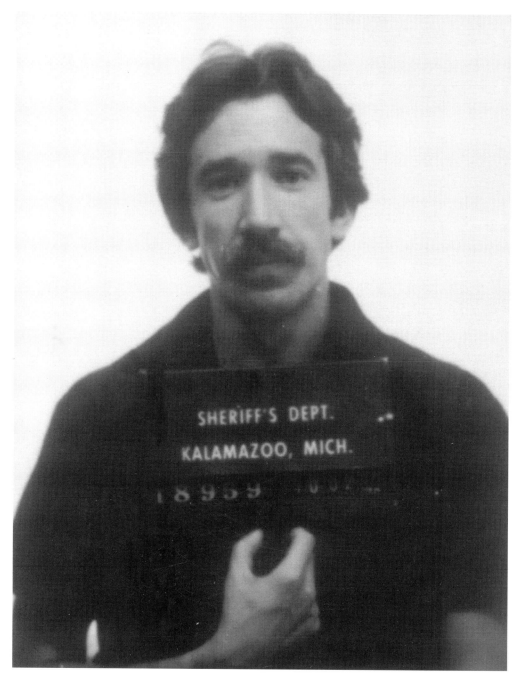

Timothy Allen Dick, who later became the popular comedian Tim Allen, after his arrest in 1978 for selling drugs.

1

"A CAULDRON OF DESPAIR"

TIM DICK LISTENED intently to the judge in the courtroom that November day in 1979. Although he heard the words, he had trouble grasping their meaning. A near-paralyzing case of nerves transformed his stomach into a churning cauldron and so numbed his muscles that he stood as if he were in a trance. He had good reason to feel uneasy: the judge's words, which in a few short moments would pronounce sentence, were directed at him.

He was only 26, not long out of college, and not yet known as the comedian Tim Allen. He had become involved in the Kalamazoo, Michigan, drug scene while attending Western Michigan University. Although he dabbled in cocaine and marijuana, his personal drug use never amounted to much. Tim was more interested in selling drugs to others for a quick profit. He knew that the drug trade could swing piles of money his way with relatively few worries—if he didn't mind the risk of getting caught.

He knew what he was doing was wrong, but it had all been so easy. After pulling off a few small deals, he was carried along by the over-

Tim had become a part of the drug scene while he was attending Western Michigan University in Kalamazoo, Michigan. After graduation, he continued to sell drugs to make "easy" money.

powering lure of big money and got sucked deeper into the shady world of illegal drugs. The drug trade was beginning to control his life.

"I knew I was doing wrong," he later told the *Washington Post.* "Immediately I wanted out of this so bad, but it's like the CIA in those old spy movies—it's real easy to get into, and it's really hard to get out."

Like many other college graduates, Tim had no idea what he wanted to do with his life. According to *Biography Today,* he drifted along without direction, but when he observed some acquaintances who were involved in the drug trade, he noticed that "the money was right. I was floundering actually. That's how I got into trouble. By 1979 I was getting very worried about where I was going."

The Michigan police were determined to make sure his destination included iron bars. For months before the arrest, Michael Pifer, an undercover narcotics state-police officer, was keeping track of Tim's movements. In August 1978, he had even purchased a few ounces of cocaine from Tim but, hoping his mark would eventually lead him to bigger dealers, held off from arresting him. However, by the end of September, Pifer told Michael Arkush in *Tim Allen Laid Bare,* he would "gain nothing further as far as locating the source or buying from the source without getting some cooperation" from Tim Dick. Pifer decided to bring in his quarry at the next opportunity.

He did not have to wait long. On October 2, Tim tossed a brown Adidas gym bag containing one-and-a-half pounds of cocaine into his Nova and drove to the Kalamazoo airport, where Pifer was waiting for him with $42,000. Tim had chosen the airport as the spot for their meeting after seeing a similar scene on television. This deal made him more uncomfortable than previous ones, however. The stakes were raised: more money was involved and the risks were greater.

When Tim and a partner arrived at the airport, they placed the cocaine in a locker and walked over to where Pifer was standing. Pifer took the locker key from Tim, walked to the locker, and removed the drugs. Suddenly, the entire area swarmed with a dozen undercover state troopers, who surrounded Tim and his partner. "The next thing I observed," Tim later told the *Detroit Free Press,* "was a gun in my face."

The officers took them to the county jail, where after being charged with delivery of a controlled substance and criminal conspiracy, Tim spent 60 terrifying days and nights awaiting his arraignment. The holding cell, with only metal benches along the walls and a toilet in the middle, contained nine other inmates. For most of his first day, Tim stayed out of the way of the other inmates, quietly hoping to be released as quickly as possible. He clung to the wall and was so petrified by his rough-looking cellmates that he wouldn't use the toilet. Eventually, Tim could wait no longer. As he stepped toward the toilet to sit down, the other men moved toward him ominously. Tim stared wide-eyed as the men drew closer, formed a circle around him, and then abruptly turned their backs to give him some privacy.

He later described his two months in the holding cell. "It's like a cauldron of despair," he told *People* magazine. Russ McQuaid, one of Tim's friends from college, visited him and later told a reporter that he came away very concerned. "He was very tense and worried, and made it clear that he had screwed up big time and really didn't know what was coming ahead of him," McQuaid said. "Most of all, I remember just the look in his eyes of being scared and in deep over his head."

Tim had every right to be frightened simply because of where he was, but when he had a few moments to think about his situation, true panic set in. Only one month before his bust, Michigan legislators, reflecting society's growing disgust with drug peddlers and users, had passed one of the nation's harshest antidrug laws. According to the new measure, anyone found guilty of selling more than a pound of cocaine faced a mandatory sentence of life in prison without parole. The stunned 25-year-old knew that he might very well spend the remainder of his life—another 50 years or so—behind bars.

Tim Dick was facing a life with no friends, no family, and no future. There would be no children to watch growing

up, no grandchildren to smother with affection. Never again would he celebrate Christmas with his mother, brothers, and sister. Never again would he go out on a date, go to the movies, or enjoy a walk in the park. The word "fear" could not begin to describe the state of Tim's mind while in the holding cell.

The ordeal was not easy for his family and friends either. William Bones, Tim's stepfather, later admitted,

One of the more popular drugs in the late 1970s was cocaine, a white powder derived from the coca leaf that causes euphoria and hallucination when inhaled or injected. Cocaine led to Tim Dick's arrest and could have ruined his life.

"None of us knew what to say. The effect he had on his mother was devastating." Some doubted if Tim could rebound sufficiently to make something of his life. Thomas Pagel, one of Tim's professors from college, told Arkush, "I felt, here's one of the most talented people I'd had and he probably would never be able to recover from it."

Fortunately, Tim's family rallied around him when he most needed them. Instead of showing shame and anger, they let Tim know he could count on them. No one yelled at Tim for being stupid or careless; no one accused anyone else of not doing enough or of not recognizing Tim's problem in time. They pulled together and found strength in one another.

Bones and Tim's mother, Martha, eventually arranged bail to get Tim out of jail until his trial. He moved back home with his parents, brothers, and sister, in Bloomfield Hills, Michigan. His parents made it clear that Tim would have to follow whatever rules they laid down. Rather than bristle at the restrictions, Tim appreciated having someone take control of his life, which had fallen into such a state of chaos that he felt he could not straighten it out without help. His family came to his rescue. In the process, Tim and his stepfather drew closer than they had ever been before.

Friends referred Tim to Jim Hills, an attorney. Tim followed Hills's advice and pleaded guilty at his arraignment. He was released on his own recognizance and returned home to await sentencing.

The eight months between his hearing and sentencing was a long time for everyone close to Tim. A particularly distasteful task for Tim was having to tell the parents of his girlfriend, Laura Deibel, what had happened. Laura's father, Gilbert Deibel, was a prominent attorney, and Tim feared a cold reaction. But the encounter passed better than expected. Although the Deibels were stunned by the news, they gave unflinching support to the man their daughter loved.

Hills, a former prosecuting attorney, knew how the system worked and suspected that the state might be interested in bigger fish than Tim. He approached the authorities with a deal, in which Tim would tell police about his drug contacts in exchange for a lighter sentence. When his proposal received a favorable response, Hills informed Tim that he might get out of this legal mess with minimum damage to his life.

Tim agreed to cooperate with the authorities and tell everything he knew about the Kalamazoo drug scene. In return, the state agreed to drop the more serious charge against him and allowed him to be sentenced in federal rather than state court, so that the judge would not be bound by Michigan's mandatory life sentence.

Although this was a good break for Tim, he still faced many unknowns. No one knew how the federal judge would rule. Although a life sentence appeared unlikely, the possibility existed that he could be sent to jail. Still, Tim did not believe he would be incarcerated. He explained in an interview later with Barbara Walters, "I never thought that I would get any time. I thought, '[I'm a] well-educated kid, I made a mistake, I admitted my error, I pleaded guilty' and that would end the matter."

Another threat loomed, however. Tim's testimony angered the drug dealers, violent men who were making vast sums of money and using strong-arm tactics to keep it. They would not take kindly to one of their own turning on them. During the eight months between his arraignment and sentencing, Tim kept a wary eye out for unfamiliar faces. Torn between two distasteful alternatives—life in prison or testifying against dangerous drug dealers—Tim chose the one that might keep him out of jail. In the process, he had placed his life in peril.

Tim's information helped the authorities indict 20 people involved in the drug trade and resulted in the conviction and sentencing of four major drug dealers. As agreed, the state dropped the charge of distributing

Tim's girlfriend, Laura Deibel, and her family were supportive after his arrest. Tim and Laura later married, and have been together nearly 20 years.

cocaine and sent Tim's case to federal court.

In hopes of convincing the judge that prison was not the proper step, Tim took a job as a salesman at the Sportsman, a Bloomfield Township sporting goods store. He and his lawyer believed this would give him more ties to the community and show he could handle responsibility. He also began to use his awakening comic talent by appearing on stage at a local comedy club, where he soon became one of the most popular acts.

Tim convinced himself that he would be placed on probation instead of sentenced to prison. In his statement to the court, he attempted to explain how he slipped into the dangerous world of drugs. After graduation, his life was without direction, and he was afraid of working and failing in the real world, he told the judge. "I became involved in this as a pretty arrogant college kid and didn't have any idea of what I was getting into," he said. Although he knew it was wrong, he started selling drugs. He said that his arrest "was the slap I kind of needed to straighten things out in my head." Being thrown into the holding cell "ended a bad ordeal, and I am glad. I want to piece myself back together and move ahead." He ended by apologizing for the discomfort he had caused. "I am really sorry for the trouble I have caused everyone, especially the mud I have pulled my parents through and stuff, but I think I can make a positive contribution to society, and I am just hoping that you look that I have no past record."

Tim's friends and family, including Laura Deibel's father, wrote lengthy letters to the court asking for leniency. Tim was a talented individual who had changed his life since his drug bust, they claimed. A college graduate who had never been in trouble before, Tim deserved a break, not a jail term. Thus, as his sentencing approached, Tim and his family felt confident he would avoid prison.

When he appeared in federal court to learn his fate, however, Tim received the surprise of his life. Instead of being swayed by the letters and by the change in Tim's life since his arrest, the federal judge handed down a five-year sentence, to be served at Sandstone Federal Correctional Institution in northern Minnesota. As his stunned mother and stepfather watched from their seats in the courtroom, federal marshals hustled Tim from the room. "The marshals grabbed him, and got him out of there, one on each side of him," recalled William Bones. "He was pretty numb at that point."

The sentence hit Tim Dick like an explosion. Within seconds his thoughts turned from the dream that his troubles would soon be over to the nightmare world of prison. "I really didn't expect that they would give me as much prison time as they did," he later told *People.* "I was a college graduate, and it looked like I'd made only one mistake. But [the judge] didn't look at it quite that way. It took so long for the idea that I was going to prison to sink in."

At least he would not be serving his time in a prison in Michigan. Concerned for Tim's safety, the judge opted for the Minnesota facility over a local prison because he feared that Tim might have some enemies there. Tim would begin serving his time after learning what his sentence would be under Michigan law the next month.

In November, Tim appeared in state court to learn what additional penalty Michigan circuit court judge Patrick Macauley might add for the state charges. Although the judge handed down another term of three to seven years, he stipulated that it was to be served concurrently with his federal sentence, meaning Tim would spend no more time behind bars than the original sentence required. He also had a powerful message for the crestfallen young man.

"Take your penalty like a man," Judge Macauley admonished Tim. "I want you to serve your time, and then get out and use your talents to assist society. You can perfect your talents while you are in prison. When you come out, I expect to see you very, very successful as a comedian. I expect to see your name in magazines. You are going to be a very successful young man."

The judge told him he had made an excellent start on correcting his life. "During the last year you have been out, you have been training. You have been perfecting your abilities. If you continue that, then this hasn't been such a tragedy. If you don't continue, if you get in with the wrong crowd, then you will have wasted all of this."

Judge Macauley included a warning he hoped the prisoner standing before him would heed seriously. "You have the unique ability to get on the stage and perform and make people smile, laugh, and be happy. That's an unusual talent. Don't waste it."

With those final words ringing in his ears, Tim Dick was led away to prison.

When Tim Dick was growing up in the 1950s, Denver, Colorado, was a small city nestled in the Rocky Mountains. Tim's family lived in Denver until he was 14 years old.

2

A GREAT CHILDHOOD

TIMOTHY ALLEN DICK was born on June 13, 1953, in Denver, Colorado, the third of five boys and one girl. He grew up in a family that seemed to mirror one of the old-time television shows where Mom and Dad had the answer to every problem and the kids worried about nothing more serious than what escapade would come next. Gerald, Tim's father, was a prominent member of Denver's insurance and real estate community; his mother, Martha, stayed home to raise the six children in the Dicks' comfortable house on Marion Street, near the posh Denver Country Club.

In summers, on weekends, and after school, Tim roamed the neighborhood and nearby fields with a group of friends who shared his love of adventure and mischief. In his autobiography, he paints a childhood out of Mark Twain's *Adventures of Tom Sawyer:* "We'd lie around on glorious summer days, blades of grass in our mouths, plotting what to do next. It was all very innocent, but the potential for trouble remained. We were tiny Neanderthals, after all."

Like many children, Tim Dick enjoyed playing "war" using toy soldiers like these. Of his childhood, Tim later wrote, "It was all very innocent, but the potential for trouble remained. We were tiny Neanderthals, after all."

Relying on bicycles for transportation, and sodas, Twinkies, and Hostess cupcakes for energy, the gang headed for the local hills or favorite hangouts to see what the day might offer. Sooner or later, they wound up at Tim's house. As one of his friends told Michael Arkush, "That's where everybody congregated. It was a major hub. We'd have sleepovers at the Dicks with eight, ten, fifteen guys. If you didn't have anything to do, you just went to the Dicks' house and knocked, and there were usually people there."

Like many boys, Tim and his friends and brothers especially loved playing war. Toy soldiers and wooden-block forts littered the basement floor, where they spent hour after hour destroying imaginary enemies and mounting large-scale attacks. When they moved the battles outside, Tim tried to be like the war character played by the actor Vic Morrow on *Combat,* a popular television series at the time, and lead his men to glorious victories. "I lived that show and I wanted to be in that squad," he writes in his autobiography. "So we put our own squads together to go against other groups."

The make-believe assaults almost led to real injury once when Tim targeted a "pillbox" made from a piano box by one of his "enemies." He grabbed a Mattel toy bazooka that launched hard plastic shells, attached a sparkler to the end, and shot the missile toward the cardboard structure. In moments, flames engulfed the pillbox, sending kids stumbling to get out. "I was the big hero because I had actually knocked out a pillbox," he later recalled. "And nearly burned and shot four children in the process."

Like many kids in that era, Tim desperately wanted his own BB gun. Naturally, his parents disapproved. When they refused to give him the money, he responded to an ad in the back of a comic book looking for people who wanted to earn money selling seeds. Although it showed initiative, he ultimately sold most of the packets to his own family, who ended up paying for the BB gun anyway.

Now armed with a weapon that propelled real ammunition, Tim stalked the neighborhood searching for targets. Most frequently, lights, windows, and cans met a quick demise, but one time he aimed at a squirrel and killed it. Feeling somehow different than he did after hitting a tin can, he next lined up a bird and dispatched it with an accurate salvo. He became so overcome with guilt that he refused to shoot any more animals.

Along with his penchant for war and marksmanship, Tim loved producing loud explosions. He and his friends would build a fortress and then demolish it with well-placed firecrackers. While this habit could be dangerous—he lost a thumbnail once when a firecracker exploded too quickly—he writes that "blowing up stuff is a rite of boyhood that continues well into manhood. We're contractors and soldiers. You can't destroy stuff unless you build it first."

Slowly, he was forming the personality and beliefs that were to emerge later in his comedy routines. Along with his fondness for military machinery, he inherited a sense of humor and a love of cars from his father. Gerald Dick livened any party he attended, and whenever Tim now cracks a joke at family gatherings, the comparisons are inevitable. Gerald's sister, Winifred Ingalls, told Arkush, "Whenever Tim says something amusing, people we grew up with even now comment at different times that Gerry would have liked that joke."

Bright, shiny cars were a staple of the Dick family, and Gerald could frequently be seen in the driveway polishing one or tinkering with another. "They always had really cool cars," a family friend told Michael Arkush. Whenever possible, Gerald piled his five sons in one of the cars and drove them to the drag races.

From his mother, Martha, Tim inherited the ability to analyze situations humorously. He remembers her saying that "men were only good for two things—lawn care and vehicle maintenance."

As Tim Dick settled comfortably into the role of the all-American boy, he experienced many awkward moments at school, mainly over his last name. Kids can be cruel, and it was a rare day he was not teased. He writes that in grade school, classmates would snicker about his unfortunate name in "the same way they giggled when they had to sing the word 'bosom' in 'The Battle Hymn of the Republic.'" Teachers seemed to pause when they read out his name in roll call.

Some people might crumble in a situation like Tim's, complaining that life is unfair or that people are cruel. Many might use the situation to rationalize cutting school or not completing assignments. Instead of making excuses and feeling sorry for himself, Tim faced the problem head-on and used the weapon that came naturally to him—humor. Rather than let it overwhelm him, he realized that if he could joke about his name first and get the other students laughing, they would stop teasing him. "For a while I hated everyone," Tim writes in his autobiography, "and the teasing caused me unnecessary grief. But in retrospect, it made me a better person." His method of dealing with the taunts worked well, and he was hooked on making people laugh. As he now bluntly asserts, "I believe my name created my life."

Soon, Tim found that not only did he have a talent for making people laugh, but he could also think quickly on his feet. No matter what a student said to him, Tim Dick came back with a better response. No one could rattle off a series of lines faster than he could. "I wasn't just going to stand there and take it, so I'd have to run through a whole routine just to defuse the situation."

Other than the flap over his last name, Tim enjoyed a typical school career. Although he never won any academic awards for his grades, he did not have to worry about failing. He kept his friends in stitches by performing hilarious imitations of other students, and he participated in more than his share of pranks.

Tim Dick could not have had a better life than the one he experienced during his childhood in Denver. In one horrifying instant, however, an event occurred that changed his idyllic existence forever.

*The Air Force–University of Colorado rivalry was the major football event in Colorado.
After the 1964 game, 11-year-old Tim's world was ripped apart when his father was
killed in a car accident on the way home.*

3

"MY WORLD CHANGED OVERNIGHT"

NINE EAGER, EXCITED people piled into the Ford station wagon. November 23, 1964, was the day the University of Colorado hosted its cross-state rival, the Air Force Academy, in what was sure to be a hard-hitting afternoon of football. Tim watched as his father and mother, two of his brothers, and five of their friends got into the car. He loved football, but today the 11-year-old preferred to stay at home with a friend. His father and mother waved goodbye and headed out onto the road.

Colorado beat its tenacious opponent in a bitterly contested 28-23 affair. After the game, Gerald Dick guided the station wagon out of the stadium's parking lot and onto the Valley Highway leading back to Denver. The traffic, heavy at first, soon thinned as cars veered off onto other highways leading home.

Suddenly, a car swerved out of control on the other side of the highway, crashed through a road sign, bounced across the median strip, and soared into the air directly toward Gerald and his eight passengers. Acting on instinct, with no thought for his own safety, Gerald jerked the wheel so that his side of the station wagon would take the full impact of the hurtling machine.

Chris Schilt, one of the family friends sitting in the back seat, looked up and saw the bottom of a car plummeting directly toward him until Gerald turned the wagon. Schilt recalled during a television documentary: "We were almost home. The car came right down on top of him and just crushed that side of the station wagon, and Gerry was killed immediately. He really took the full brunt of the car." Schilt added that if Gerald had delayed for even a moment, the careening car would have crushed the back half of the station wagon, injuring or killing the children inside.

Gerald's heroics saved the other passengers, but he could not protect himself from the tragic consequences of a car driven out of control by a drunk driver. He was active in city affairs and president of the Denver Insurers Association; his funeral at Ascension Church drew hundreds of mourners.

His children, shocked by this tragic turn of events, wondered how something like this could happen. Tim struggled with the thought that his decision to stay home saved his life. He later said, "I would have sat where I usually sit [next to his father] and it crushed his side of the car and I would have died." As it was, Tim was suddenly forced to face life as an 11-year-old without a father. "He had a carload of people, including my mom and all my brothers," Tim told *People,* "and he was the only one killed."

Bewildered by the loss of his father, Tim found it difficult to grieve. Instead of venting his feelings, he locked them tightly inside. He understood all too well that his world had changed drastically. Years later, he wrote, "This loss stretched every boundary I knew. I wasn't king of my universe anymore. In fact, I felt helpless, useless, pathetic. I had no control, and my scramble to regain some made me grow up very quickly."

Tim compared his father's death to "earthquakes; things that shake your foundation. . . . All of a sudden my world changed overnight. One day he was there, and the next he was gone." The boy felt vulnerable now. "I realized there is no one here to protect us; that life can be taken from us at any time. Life is a great gift. God is to be both loved and tremendously feared. And the balance between the two is what it's all about."

The burden of raising five boys and one girl now fell solely on the shoulders of Tim's mother. She was able to show a toughness and durability that held them together in these trying months. One month after the funeral, she took all the children to Michigan, where she grew up. There, surrounded by family and comforted by friends, she and her children could start the healing process.

Whenever possible, they went to Michigan and familiarity. On one of these trips, Martha rekindled her interest in a high school sweetheart, William Bones, who had since risen to an executive position with RCA. Like Martha, he too had lost his spouse in an automobile accident. Left alone with three children of his own to raise, William Bones needed Martha as much as she needed him.

It proved to be a blessing, although at the time Tim and his siblings were feeling mixed emotions. When their mother and William Bones announced their intention to marry in 1966, the children were pleased for their mother but anxious about their own situations. Having lost a father only three short years before, they now had to leave Denver, their childhood friends, and all the memories associated with that beautiful mountain location, and move somewhere else, where they would have to adjust to life with a new father and new brothers and sisters.

Martha and her children moved to the Detroit area at one of the most turbulent times in that city's history.

Racial tensions that split the metropolitan area into two segments flared in the violent summer riots that plagued not only Detroit but other large cities across the nation. Although the family would be living in the affluent suburb of Birmingham, where the shining cars and expansive homes created a world totally opposite from Detroit, the

After her husband's death, Tim's mother married her high school sweetheart and moved the family from the beautiful natural surroundings of Colorado to a major industrial center: Detroit, Michigan.

thought of moving filled Tim and the others with unease.

Tim later told the *Detroit Free Press* that the move was "traumatic. And we moved from the mountains and streams of Colorado, in its heyday, to Detroit, just before the summer of 1967. It was a strange time to move. I was going, 'Gosh, look: tanks. I'm going to like this place.'"

Tim Allen signs copies of his best-selling 1994 book Don't Stand Too Close to a Naked Man. *In the book, which was dedicated to his stepfather, Tim humorously recalled his years growing up in Detroit and Denver.*

Making the situation even more complicated was the fact that Tim had to get used to a new father. William Bones handled the delicate situation with compassion, but he had the wisdom and experience of years. Tim had neither. As he explained to *Biography Today*, "My stepfather came in when I was at that obstinate stage. We had problems getting on the right track."

Tim adjusted to school more easily than he did to home life. Nevertheless, because he was the new kid in school and had an odd last name, some problems were bound to surface. All through his four years at Birmingham Seaholm High School he belonged to a group of students who were popular and liked to have a good time.

Classmate Michael Souter told Arkush, "We never did anything that I would call bad. We kept the teachers going. I think they were sad when we left because we were always doing something."

Like many other teenage boys, Tim loved cars. Shop class was his favorite period of the school day, and at night he often accompanied friends to Woodward Avenue, a wide street where they would drag race. When it came to girls and dating, however, Tim's confidence flew out the window. The shy youth dated, but he did not feel comfortable around girls. As Tim later wrote, "I figured that flirting was about as far as I was going to get, anyway, since I had such a horrible complexion."

What distinguished Tim most during this period was his humor. Everybody loved following him around to hear his next outrageous line. He used humor when he had to—to defuse the taunting he suffered over his last name—but students and friends began to appreciate his sharp wit for what it was.

Classmate Amy Hursley recalled, "He used to do a lot of skits." Tim would "start making tons and tons of jokes, and they would all kind of roll together. You were just completely outwitted all the way through." Some might try to top his humor, she recalled, but once Tim got going the challengers would "have to walk away because there was nothing more that you could do." Tim's ability to imitate others, especially females, kept his friends in stitches. His talent for making people laugh, Tim said in a documentary, came from his father. "I believe I got my sense of humor from him."

Tim used that humor to mask the pain he still felt over his father's death and the family's subsequent move to Michigan. Rather than face his painful feelings, he avoided them by joking around and being the center of attention. His mother told the *Detroit Free Press* that, in this way, Tim was "like his father. He used humor to cover up his emotions."

Gradually, Tim drew closer to his stepfather. As William Bones had known Martha since high school, their stability helped soothe a tumultuous situation for the nine children who now had to learn to live together. Tim so appreciated the love and kindness that William Bones brought to the marriage that he wrote of his mother and stepfather, "Their love rescued us all." In 1994, when he was dedicating his first book, *Don't Stand Too Close to a Naked Man,* Tim wrote, "For my new dad, Bill, who stepped up to the plate and hit a home run for all of us."

Although Tim was chosen to be master of ceremonies for the senior class's popular talent show "Swingout!" and distinguished himself as the class clown, he did not go around telling everyone that a Hollywood career beckoned. Not particularly focused, Tim seemed to drift along with the crowd, content to entertain people with his jokes. Unlike others who eventually found success in sports, politics, or entertainment by planning, studying hard, and working toward a defined goal, Tim had no such plan. His grades rarely made the school's honor rolls; his teachers never thought he was a surefire bet to succeed.

Some people need time and experience before they are ready to begin their life's quest. By the time he graduated from Birmingham Seaholm in 1971, Tim Dick possessed the fundamentals for a career as an entertainer, but he lacked the focus and the drive to chase after his dream.

Nevertheless, he knew his future lay in comedy. One day Tim told a friend, "Someday I'm going to be on the Johnny Carson show," a popular late-night television talk show that featured up-and-coming comedians.

Bubbling somewhere inside Tim, barely recognizable, was this love of humor and a desire to forge a career in entertainment. Perhaps in college his dream would begin to take shape.

When Tim Allen was in college, his dream was to appear on The Tonight Show *with Johnny Carson.*

4

"HE'S JUST A JOKER"

SITUATED BEYOND MILES of rolling farmland in the small town of Mount Pleasant, 150 miles northwest of Detroit, is Central Michigan University, where Tim spent the first two years of his college life. Rather than concentrate on his class assignments, however, he moved from party to party with his friends from his old high school.

There was not much to do at Central on the weekends, so everyone headed elsewhere for fun. Mark Klepper, Tim's roommate in his sophomore year, told Arkush, "It seemed like we were always going someplace. There was nothing to do at Central. It was in the middle of nowhere."

Although Tim was developing his social skills far more than his academic prowess, he nevertheless exhibited traces of what his future might hold. Klepper recalled that they frequently watched *The Tonight Show with Johnny Carson,* and that Tim "always kind of talked about being a Johnny Carson." According to Klepper, many times Tim boasted that "I could do that as good as he's [Carson] doing that."

Tim transferred to another college after his second year to pursue a growing interest in acting. Western Michigan University, in Kalamazoo,

was known for its excellent television production department. It also had a reputation for its social life—so much so that one magazine rated it the nation's number-one party school. Tim had the opportunity to attend challenging, stimulating classes; he also had the opportunity to attend nonstop parties where drugs were passed around freely.

He tried to manage both worlds. Professors admired his insights, concepts that other students often missed. Jules Rossman, who taught a commercial-writing course, said

After two years of college at Central Michigan University, Tim transferred to Western Michigan University. The school's television production curriculum, which Tim decided to study, had an excellent reputation—but Western Michigan was also considered a "party school," and Tim fell in with a wild group of friends.

later that Tim's scripts "were always far superior to anybody else's as far as creativity, originality, and humor. He had that spark of difference about him."

Communications professor Thomas Pagel soon recognized great potential in his student. Pagel was so impressed with one project Tim created that he saved a videotape of the work, thinking his student might be famous one day. The skit concerned a male student who has a crush on a girl and, believing she felt the same about

*When Tim graduated in 1976,
he did not use his new degree
to find a job in television.
Instead, he was lured by the
fun of nightlife and parties
into a world of drugs, money,
and danger.*

him, approaches her. Instead of getting a date, however, the student awkwardly learns that she already has a boyfriend.

Although Tim Dick may not have been aware of it, he was already beginning to explore a theme that he, first as Tim Allen and then as his television character Tim Taylor, would ride to fame: the inability of men and women to understand each other. Professor Pagel said to one writer, Tim "seemed always to be a bit intrigued and bemused about relationships between men and women. He was interested in the failures of communication, and he wanted to dramatize it somehow."

Professor Pagel told reporter Marc Gunther of the *Detroit Free Press* that "Tim, very early, showed a lot of ability. His work for me in performance was really quite exceptional." To another writer, Pagel reported that he "saw much of what there is now, the kind of playfulness and sense of telling with his face what he's feeling inside." Pagel also remarked that Tim "seemed to need the attention" that came with performing.

Pagel noticed that Tim tried to appear less clever than he actually was. "He played down his intellectual capacity. He tried to slough it off that he really didn't care all that much, and yet, when the work would come in, it would be generally better than you would expect."

Pagel gave Tim an A for the course. Tim's talent was beginning to demonstrate itself, but he had a long way to go and many hardships to endure before realizing success.

No matter what he achieved at Western Michigan University, Tim has always been grateful to his alma mater, because he met his future wife there.

Never comfortable around women, Tim was more at ease flirting with them and making them laugh; few saw him as anything more than a funny guy going nowhere. His roommate, Mark Klepper, said that Tim "was one that girls wanted to be around, but not necessarily the one that somebody would settle down with because, at that point, they'd be thinking, 'What's this guy going to do? He's just a joker.'"

Tim once had such a deep crush on a girl that he followed her back to her dormitory to see where she lived. He looked up her class schedule and found out where she worked. But, as he writes in his autobiography, if he was going to meet her, "I would have to step in front of her and say hello." He never built up enough courage to take that step. "I always chickened out."

One girl gradually began to occupy more of his time. Laura Deibel, the daughter of a prominent lawyer from Saginaw, Michigan, possessed a sense of humor that blended perfectly with Tim's. The two clicked from the start. As William Bones told a Los Angeles reporter, "They were very comfortable with each other, and they confided in each other. They discussed things you wouldn't normally do if it were just a date."

Tim did not spend every spare moment with Laura, however. To sharpen his comedic skills, he worked with a group of other students at the campus radio station. Each week, six or seven students wrote, organized, and broadcast a half-hour comedy radio show. The more controversial the person or topic they poked fun at, the more Tim and his friends enjoyed it. Nothing was sacred. The students earned a reputation for wit and daring, and the show had a loyal following.

"We were all pretty quick guys because all of us had either gone into media or advertising, but it seemed like Tim was always about half a beat faster than everybody else," fellow radio comedian Russ McQuaid told a reporter years later. "His comedic view of life was skewed toward the absurd. He'd see the hypocrisy in things." McQuaid later added, "You could tell from being with him that, hopefully, this [his talent] was not going to stop here, and that he'd find some way to make big money someday."

By the time he graduated in 1976 with a bachelor's degree in television production, Tim Dick had made a mark in his field. Everyone on campus recognized his talent. Everyone knew that if the breaks went the right way, Tim could go far in entertainment.

Instead of perfecting that talent, however, Tim fell in with the wrong crowd and plunged deeper into a world of drugs, money, and danger. Over the next two years, he earned a few dollars as a freelance artist, but mostly he made a living selling marijuana. He was still drifting along, waiting for something to happen instead of taking the initiative and making something happen.

"I was a graduate with no direction," he rationalized at his trial for selling cocaine. "Since my father was killed, I have not been directed and I had trouble taking things seriously. I was afraid of working and failing in the real world." As a result, he added, "I ended up in a continued fantasy—drugs. At the time, it was very 'chic' to have and use coke. Record shops had the neat supplies, new wave magazines extolled its virtues, and I became wrapped up [in] the cocaine cult."

It was a cult that nearly destroyed Tim Dick's world before it ever began.

Tim Allen delivers his stand-up routine during a television special. He took his first steps toward a career in comedy after his arrest for selling drugs. While he was awaiting sentencing, he gave his first stand-up performance on February 12, 1979.

5

A FLOOR TILE
FROM RIDLEY'S

AFTER HIS ARREST for drug dealing and his two-month stay in the holding cell, Tim Dick awaited his sentencing at home with his mother and stepfather. He took a job as a sporting-goods salesman in an effort to show the judge that he had "gone clean," but as sometimes occurs with individuals on their way to fame, an unexpected incident happened that profoundly influenced the young man and edged him further onto the entertainment route.

A Detroit-area stand-up comic named Eric Head came into the store one day, and Tim waited on him. It wasn't long before Head found himself laughing out loud as this clerk fired off a series of one-liners. Head remained in the store for four hours listening to Tim's wry observations. "I thought he was about the funniest guy I had ever met," he recalled later. "I wasn't used to being waited on with such irreverence and sarcasm. It just killed me. I loved it."

Near the end of their lengthy meeting, Head challenged his new friend to go onstage. "If I could do this," he urged, "you could certainly do it. You're a real funny guy. You better do it, because you're going to make a mistake if you don't."

Mark Ridley, the owner of the first comedy club in Detroit, gave Tim his first break as a stand-up comedian. After learning about Tim's trouble with the law, Ridley assured the young comedian that he would have a job at his club after he got out of jail.

Tim mentioned that he had given the idea some thought, so the two started going to Detroit's comedy hub, Mark Ridley's Room of Comedy and Magic. Opened in the late 1970s in the basement of a local restaurant, the nightspot offered local comedians a chance to try out their material and acquire valuable experience in front of a live audience. Later renamed the Comedy Castle, it was the first Detroit comedy club and the forerunner of many such clubs that would flourish in the 1980s around the country.

Tim, Eric Head, and other friends watched various comedians perform at Ridley's. One comedian was Dave Coulier, who would eventually land his own television series. After every routine, Tim would mutter, "I could do that. I'm funnier than those guys." And Head would fire back another challenge for Tim to climb onstage and prove it. As Tim later told the *Detroit Free Press,* "He finally snapped my cord. I went down to my basement and just wrote 30 minutes."

On February 12, 1979, the night of Timothy Allen Dick's first public performance, the hopeful comedian battled a severe case of stage fright just before he was announced. Mark Ridley told *Time,* "He was a bundle of nerves, shaking his hands and pacing himself into a frenzy. But boom, once he was up there, he was in control." To this day, before each performance, Tim nervously paces back and forth until the show begins.

He used the name Tim Allen so the audience would not be distracted by his real last name. Tim figured that if he could face a possible life sentence, he could certainly cope with an audience. As he told the *Detroit Free Press,* "I had a guillotine on my neck. So, why not? I've got nothing to lose." For his debut performance, Tim put on a blue suit and red tie (unusual wear for most comedians) and drove to the club with his younger brother, Bruce.

Tim's comedy routine included jokes about bees and a bit about baking the Pillsbury dough boy. The first five minutes seemed endless as the audience sat in silence.

Beads of perspiration dotted Tim's forehead as he imagined his career as a comedian ending before it had begun. Then one of his jokes got a few laughs. The next joke got a few more. As the laughter became louder, Tim's confidence increased. He finished his act and walked off the stage to a round of applause.

Tim wasn't sure of his performance, and quickly asked his brother, "Was I funny?"

"You were all right," Bruce replied, "but did you have to sweat so much?"

Mark Ridley had no doubts. He told Tim that, for a debut act, he had done a great job. "I asked him if he wanted

After his first performance at Mark Ridley's Room of Comedy and Magic (later renamed Mark Ridley's Comedy Castle), Tim dug a tile out of the floor, wrote the date on the tile, and took it with him as a keepsake of the day his career began.

to do some more. Tim said yes." Pleased to be asked back, Tim felt he had to be honest and open with Ridley: "There are two things I need to tell you. My real name is Tim Dick, and I'm going to jail." Ridley told him he was welcome to perform until he left for jail, and a spot would be waiting for him after he had served his time. "We were so new then that if somebody got laughs, they were brilliant," Ridley explained to the *Detroit Free Press.*

Tim had succeeded in entertaining a live audience. He was hooked. The college student who drifted about without goals or ambitions was now a determined comedian out to carve a niche for himself in the world of show business. He understood the significance of that night's performance. When no one was looking, Tim took a quarter from his pocket, dug out the grout from the floor near the bar, and removed one of the floor tiles. He wrote the date—February 12, 1979—on the tile and took it with him as a keepsake. That piece of tile from Ridley's club still hangs on the wall in Tim Allen's office.

Over the next eight months, Tim Allen became a familiar name at the club. His routine improved with each performance, and fans began coming to the club just to catch his act. Fellow comedian Tim Lilly later said, "Tim came right out of the box as one of the stronger acts in town."

The night before he was to begin his jail sentence, Tim gave one last performance and then made some brief goodbyes. Ridley and a few select friends knew about Tim's trouble with the law, but most of the other comedians had no idea until later. Tim simply told the other comedians he would see them sometime soon. "He sort of took it in good spirits," said Ridley. "There wasn't crying and hugging. He wanted to keep it kind of low-key."

Tim had changed since his arrest. Although he was still terrified of going to jail, he now had something waiting for him on his release. Ridley's promise to save a spot for him instilled a new confidence in Tim. In a television interview, Ridley said, "All he talked about [the night before entering jail] was he couldn't wait to get back and be onstage again."

Combined with the love and loyalty of his girlfriend, Laura, and the support of his close-knit family, Tim's eagerness to return to performing gave him something to look forward to. He had love, he had support, and he had a future. All he had to do now was get through prison.

The 18 months Tim Dick spent in prison were probably the most trying time of the young comedian's life.

6

"THE BIG KICK"

SANDSTONE FEDERAL CORRECTIONAL Institution in Sandstone, Minnesota, was Tim Allen's new home for the indeterminate future. It was a low-security facility that housed a few hundred inmates. Most of the men weren't murderers or rapists, but they were still scary enough to intimidate a sheltered boy from the suburbs.

Tim soon learned two tricks that helped him endure his time inside. First, if another prisoner bothered him, he started acting crazy, shouting (according to what high school friend Rick Bach told Michael Arkush), "If you touch me, I'm going to have to kill you, or at least die trying." The second was the talent that held hope for him after jail: his sense of humor. As Tim told *People,* "Humor was the only defense I had. Two minutes after I was there, I started babbling. So everyone knew I was a geek right away."

He made the guards laugh by putting pictures of former president Richard Nixon in his cell's peephole. He made fellow inmates howl by supplying a steady stream of jokes and one-liners. In effect, prison put Tim Allen onstage around the clock.

One muscular prisoner kept threatening to beat him up. He had no particular reason, according to Tim, other than "just because he could. Just because he was bored." But when Tim slipped into his Elmer Fudd imitation, saying, "Yeah, it's pwetty cwose to cwosin' time," the tough guy would practically fall over laughing and then walk away. As Tim related, "You could kick butt anytime. But you don't get to laugh that much in prison. It proved very valuable to me."

Locked away for possibly as long as seven years, Tim made the best of a bad situation. Many men there fared very poorly. Tim saw "a sadness inside those walls, in men's eyes, that's pathetic. The loneliness. The anger. It was incredible." Tim turned his prison time into a positive experience by working on his stand-up routine and by reading and writing.

In prison, Tim had—literally—a captive audience for his comedy. He wrote material and then tried it out on small groups of inmates. He even managed to convince prison officials to allow him and Mark Kornhauser, a visiting comedian-magician from outside, to stage a show.

The event may have helped satisfy Tim's yearning to appear before a live audience again, but it did not go over well. Tim had written an evening's worth of material about prison life, hoping that the familiar would be funny, but he misjudged his audience. As Kornhauser told a Los Angeles reporter, "The prisoners didn't really like it at all. It was a little too close to home for them to laugh at it. It's possible you can laugh at something like that if you know you're getting out in a while, but some of those guys were in for life. They were pretty hardcore. I think had he done a normal stand-up routine, Tim would have done much better."

The audience stared back at Tim in silence. "He was squirming," remembered Kornhauser. "He very early recognized that they weren't buying this, yet he was committed to do what he had written, and had to go ahead with it."

While Tim was in prison, he learned that a friend from the Detroit comedy club scene, Dave Coulier, had earned a role on a television show. This made Tim more determined to get out of jail and become a success.

Tim "bombed" (as they say in show business), but the show gave him a chance to perform and strengthened his desire to become a comedian.

When Kornhauser left, Tim walked with him partway through the prison, toward the exit doors. As Kornhauser stepped through, Tim had to step back. "This big iron door slid between us," Kornhauser remembers. "He was on one side and I was on the other, and he looked so forlorn. It was very sad."

Tim joined a prison group called the Toastmaster's Club, which helps teach inmates how to speak well in public. The night Tim was being installed as new president of the group and the outgoing president was being honored, Tim stood up and started to "roast" his predecessor. As the other man silently listened, Tim poked fun at him in front of everyone.

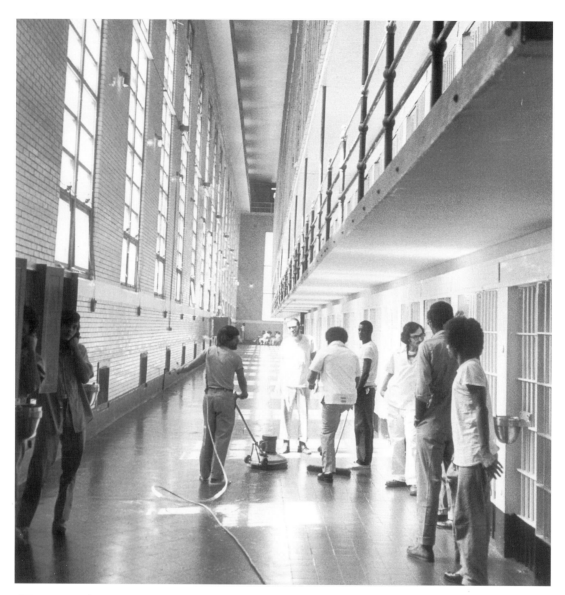

"Prison was the worst and best thing that ever happened to me," Tim Allen wrote in his book Don't Stand Too Close to a Naked Man. *"It taught me in no uncertain terms to be responsible for my own actions."*

It was all in good fun, but not for the guy who was the butt of Tim's humor. Later that night, he barged into Tim's cell, told him he hated to be criticized, and that he was in jail because he was not well balanced. He accused Tim of making him look foolish in front of the others. "And for that you're going to have to pay."

The inmate lunged at Tim, grabbing him by the shirt collar. As Tim recounts the event in his autobiography, "You could hear me gulp in the warden's office. In a split second, he got me up against a wall. I realized I was going to die." Then Tim had an idea. He saw, in his mind's eye, his brother laughing at him when they were mountain climbing as boys. Tim had lost his grip, and as he began slipping, there was a look of complete panic on his face. As his brother looked down at the helpless Tim, he burst out laughing. "The look on your face as you were sliding off that rock killed me!" his brother told him afterward.

The memory of that incident made Tim laugh. When the inmate asked him what was so funny, Tim couldn't explain. The angry prisoner loosened his grip, shook his head, and walked away, amazed that someone about to be beaten senseless could laugh about it. "You're crazy," he called back to Tim.

Tim kept in touch with the comedians he knew outside prison. Once a month, he telephoned Mark Ridley to find out which comics were doing well. He was pleased—albeit a little envious—when he learned that Dave Coulier had landed a key role in a television series. It made him more determined to reach the top.

He also wrote to Eric Head, one of the few comedians who corresponded regularly with Tim during his incarceration. He and Eric hoped to form a large production company that would make movies and television shows. They wrote about what their plush offices would look like. As Eric told Michael Arkush, "We said we wanted the hippest lobby in the world. It would not have any chairs to sit in, a male secretary at a podium, and we thought that would be the ultimate, that you'd have no place to sit when you came in."

These letters from Eric helped Tim get through his time in prison. He never lacked the support of his friends or doubted his family's loyalty. His mother told *Time,* "Tim accepted [his prison sentence]. He knew he deserved it,

Tim used his time in prison to determine his future goals and focus on them, enrolling in prison classes and attending a rehabilitation program. "I used the facilities of prison to figure out what was important and moved on from there," Tim said later. Many prisons offer classes so that inmates can learn a job skill to use after they are released. This inmate in a Massachusetts prison is learning carpentry through one of these rehabilitation programs.

and he didn't fight it. Everyone in the family came out and rallied behind him."

Laura also stayed in Tim's corner. She could have gone back to Saginaw, met a high-profile attorney or businessman, and lived a full life, but she didn't. As she said to *USA Today,* "I never even considered the other option [to leave]. It was just the right thing to do." In an interview with *People,* she explained her feelings in very straightforward terms: "We loved each other. It was that simple."

No matter how strong his support from the outside world, nothing would have helped unless Tim gained something positive from his incarceration. Many inmates, he noticed, were angry deep inside and resented what they considered society's unfair treatment of them. Tim knew not to fall into that trap. He enrolled in prison classes, attended a rehabilitation program even though he had stopped using drugs, and tried to maintain a healthy outlook.

Possessed of a quick, analytical mind, Tim had never turned it to his advantage until now. He read many books, thought about the lack of direction in his life, and tried to evaluate where he had been and where he was going. In the process, he started to learn about himself.

"It was frightening, that whole time, how much anger I had," he told *Time* later. "Then the anger was directed toward me, so I had to take the blame for this whole situation I put myself into." Instead of blaming parents, teachers, or society for his predicament, Tim placed the responsibility squarely on his own shoulders. "Prison was the worst and the best thing that ever happened to me," he writes in his autobiography. "It taught me in no uncertain terms to be responsible for my own actions."

Through this process of intense self-evaluation, Tim realized that, although he had been a drifter so far in life, he actually possessed an inner toughness that enabled him to survive difficult situations. He confided to *TV Guide,* "There are obvious dangers in prison, but I wasn't as weak as I thought I was. I got through it."

He began to take pride in small things. When he was moved out of a cell block into his own cubicle, according to his autobiography, Tim took his first look and said, "'Wow! My own room, my own toilet! And two storage lockers.' It was still the size of a bathroom in a New York luxury apartment, but I was in heaven." Then he called his mother to tell her the good news, as though he had just been given an award.

"I said, 'Mom! Mom! Guess what?' She said, 'What's wrong?' because I wasn't calling at my usual time." When he told her, she replied, "Oh, I'm so proud." Tim knew that while he was raving about his new digs, his brothers and sisters were graduating from college, embarking upon successful careers, and starting families. Compared to this, his news placed him somewhat lower on his mother's list of things to brag about. He knew she would not be running around the neighborhood telling everyone that her son had just been given his very own cell in federal prison, but he was pleased nevertheless with his accomplishment.

Most important, Tim was beginning to see for the first time how unfocused and aimless his life had been. He had already come to that conclusion when it was reinforced by another inmate. Tim wrote that before he went to jail, "I had no idea about looking forward and setting a goal. Then I met a guy in prison, at one of these groups, who summed it up best. The greatest missile in the world is useless, he said, unless it's targeted. A torpedo is adrift unless it has someplace to go. An arrow is pointless unless it hits something."

The prisoner's comments hit their mark. Tim Allen came away from the group session with a keener awareness of himself. "So it's important for kids—for everyone, even if you fail at first—to target something and head in that direction. With all your might."

This one thought made Tim's long months in prison worthwhile. It was an idea he held on to as he embarked on a road strewn with the names of those who had tried and failed at a career in show business. He later told *USA Today,* "In a hideous way, aside from the pain it put my family and friends through, getting caught [selling drugs] probably saved my life. I used the facilities of prison to figure out what was important and moved on from there."

Tim feels some other power may have played a role in his life. "I'm a firm believer in destiny," he told the *Detroit Free Press.* "I have been since I was a kid. There was a very dark path ahead of me. I needed the big hand of God to be raised and say, 'Look, you have better things in store for you.' Most people don't have that chance." As he told another reporter, "Being in a penitentiary realigned everything. Sometimes you have to hit bottom to know where to go."

Michael Souter, Tim's friend from high school, told Michael Arkush, "Prison gave him the big kick. Tim always did a lot of stuff in college, but he never had the big kick. We were all taken care of by our parents. We did things to a certain extent, but we never had to fight real hard for them. We just took a lot for granted."

In February 1981, after 18 months in jail, Tim learned that he would be released from Sandstone and placed in a halfway house in downtown Detroit, across the street from Tiger Stadium. Although he was free to resume his fledgling comedy career, the government would keep him on a short tether for the next five years: he was on parole.

Before Tim entered prison, no passion stirred him, no goal lit a fire in him to work hard and persevere. By the start of 1981, however, Tim knew exactly what he wanted; he knew, too, that he would sacrifice anything to get there. He was certain that obstacles would stand in his way, but he had survived a stretch in prison. How much tougher could show business be? A different Tim Allen emerged from the Sandstone Federal Correctional Institution, one filled with desire and promise.

Tim Allen sits at a tool bench. After his release from jail and his return to performing stand-up comedy, Tim built a career from his love of tools and machinery.

7

"LET'S GET IN THE GARAGE, GUYS!"

IN THE HALFWAY house, Tim was freer than he had been for the last year and a half, but he was still far from being a free man. He could leave each morning, hold different jobs, and mingle with his friends, but he had to be back every night by a certain time or face the threat of jail again. The halfway house was no resort hotel either. Tim's stepfather, William Bones, told Michael Arkush, "It was a very grim place. It was kind of dark and dingy, in an old building, in not the best part of Detroit."

Tim first set out to restore the connections with his previous employer, the owner of the Sportsman. Not the most exciting job in town, nor the highest paying, at least it was something with which Tim was familiar. Once he felt more comfortable with his transition out of prison, he could move on to bigger challenges, but for now the Sportsman fit perfectly.

Tim supplemented his sales job writing advertising copy. Former high school friends Rick Bach and Donald O'Connor owned a Detroit-area advertising agency; they asked Tim to create scripts for

Tim's friend Eric Head helped him to land work as a television pitchman for Bob's Big Boy, Kmart, and other companies.

slide presentations for Uniroyal Tires. He also began to act in commercials for Ford, Chevrolet, and Kmart.

Tim also landed television spots through his association with Eric Head, who had become an account manager for a large advertising agency. Tim appeared as a spokesman for Big Boy restaurants, Action Auto, Tuffy Mufflers, and Pella Windows. Soon, he could add to his resumé a list of more than 500 commercials he had either written, produced, or performed in.

Although he was earning more money and gaining valuable experience, Tim lived with the fear that his prison record was hanging over his head like a sword, waiting to destroy his dreams. Eric quietly hired Tim without informing his agency that his friend had only recently been released from prison. He believed in Tim and took a gamble that no one would uncover the truth. Eric explained to Michael Arkush: "I wouldn't dare tell my boss that I was about to put a guy who had just gotten out of prison in a series of six or seven commercials representing our biggest account. I purposely kept that confidential. When you're trying to sell a client on a spokesperson, you don't lead off with, 'He just got out of the slammer.' So Tim and I kept that to ourselves."

Head's strategy worked. Still, Tim never knew when someone would dig up his past and use it against him. He had paid for his crime by serving his jail sentence. Would he have to pay a heavier price later on, by watching his hopes slip through his fingers? He waited. In jail, Tim had decided to take responsibility for his actions; this was a consequence that one day he might have to face.

There was a packed house the night Tim returned to the Comedy Castle to resume his stand-up career. The audience was composed mostly of fellow comedians eager to see if Tim had lost his touch. To their surprise, they saw he had improved.

Comedian Tony Hayes saw Tim that night and remarked to a reporter, "It was like he had never left. He was a little rusty but he still had that sense of humor. He actually had a better act when he got out of prison."

Tim started out at the Comedy Castle as the opening act for out-of-town comedians. Before long he had so firmly established himself that the other comedians asked Ridley not to put Tim on before them; they knew he would be such a hit with the audience that they couldn't top him. Tim began appearing in other nightclubs and soon rose to become one of Michigan's top stand-up comedians.

This was not enough for the ambitious entertainer, whose sights were set on Hollywood. Every time fellow comedian Dave Coulier visited from Los Angeles, Tim grew more determined to follow in his footsteps. One day, he too would appear on *The Tonight Show* and make it to the top.

After a few months, Tim was released from the halfway house. He now had the freedom to leave the state of Michigan and take his act to other parts of the country. He still had to check in with his parole officer, but he could do that by telephone. His success allowed him to quit his jobs with the advertising agencies and the Sportsman. Tim was now ready to take his act on the road.

By 1985, Tim was flying to Hollywood often, trying to get noticed by performing in comedy clubs and making commercials.

By 1985, Tim started flying out to the West Coast every few months, trying to break into Hollywood by appearing in commercials or comedy clubs. He wasn't having much luck in Los Angeles, but his popularity in Michigan continued to flourish. Tim never turned down an invitation to further his career, whether from a shopping mall, small club, or local cable television show. After doing his act on a low-budget dance show, Tim told his surprised friends, "Look, man, it's TV."

In 1982, he appeared on a Detroit television talk show as a "chocologist," a scientist who studies the various uses of chocolate. In the middle of the playoffs during the 1984 baseball season, when everyone in Detroit was home watching the Tigers, Tim took a job at a local Holiday Inn. The night was eminently forgettable. As he later told the *Detroit Free Press*, "Seven people are in this bar, the Tigers are winning, and I'm standing next to the seven-foot screen with the game turned up loud."

While Tim was trying to do his routine, someone yelled "Shhhhh."

While Tim was perfecting his act, he knew that if he were to make it to the big time, he would need something special—a hook—to lift him above the hundreds of other comedians. He had to find a distinguishing feature that audiences would identify with Tim Allen.

Tim began to wonder if he would ever rise above the local comedy scene. He wasn't making much money. Laura was a sales design representative and was good at it; he was relying on her for financial help, which bothered him. According to the *Detroit Free Press,* he once asked a friend, in desperation, "Am I ever going to make any money? I'm tired of having Laura support me."

The year 1984 was a turning point for Tim. He and Laura married, and Tim stumbled onto his comedy hook. It happened at a nightclub in Akron, Ohio. Akron is a city so identified with automobiles and tires—the world headquarters for several major tire companies dot the landscape—that it's called the rubber capital of the world. The Goodyear Tire and Rubber Company was hosting a male-only entertainment night at the club for its employees, and Tim was hired to provide some laughs.

He opened with his usual material, but nothing seemed to work. The men were too busy eating food and talking to each other to care what some unknown comic was talking about. Tim quickly realized he had to do something to attract their attention. He told *Biography Today:* "I said, 'Let's get in the garage, guys!' And I started this run about tools and pliers and dadohead cutting. And they just went 'Yaaah!' and listened to me."

He talked about going to Sears to buy tools, and about working on cars. He made grunts that sounded like a Neanderthal man waking from a long sleep. With each grunt, the laughter and applause grew more vociferous. That night in Akron, Ohio, Tim found the hook he believed would give him the edge.

He returned home to work on his new routine. In the following months, he sharpened his act so that the name "Tim Allen" would be unmistakably linked with tools, cars, and "men's stuff." The basis of his routine, he told *Biography Today,* was to glorify the male world without being insulting to women. "I have a very feminist upbringing, and I wish there was a thing called 'masculinist.'" His comedy, he continued, is "a celebration of men's stuff: Gunk, gaskets, Lava soap, aluminum boats, bass fishing, big V-8s, blowing your nose with your thumb over a nostril. . . . It doesn't represent anything antiwoman, it's just things women would never, ever think of doing or enjoying. And these things make women laugh, because they're just hysterically stupid. They go, 'If this is all you want, go ahead.'"

Tim says that men love tools because they are "weapons for pacifists"; they allow men to attack something, even tear it down, without harming anyone. He told *Popular Mechanics,* "I'm a nut about building things. I've always loved the before-and-after process." He says that some psychologists claim men love building things because they cannot give birth to babies. Although he likes that notion, he points out a crucial distinction: "a baby will wake you at 3 A.M., a do-it-yourself project will keep you awake until 3 A.M."

Along with their love for tools and machines, Tim talks in his act about men's most perplexing problem: women. In his autobiography he writes, "Women are not the opposite sex, they're a whole other species." He builds his humor on the fact that many males think they have found the solution to the riddle of the female, but sooner or later they realize they have been spinning in circles. Women are like golf: "With both, the mystery is never revealed. Right when you think you've got it, you suddenly feel like a beginner. However, the illusion that we can plumb the mystery of woman remains."

Although he built his act around the simple love a man

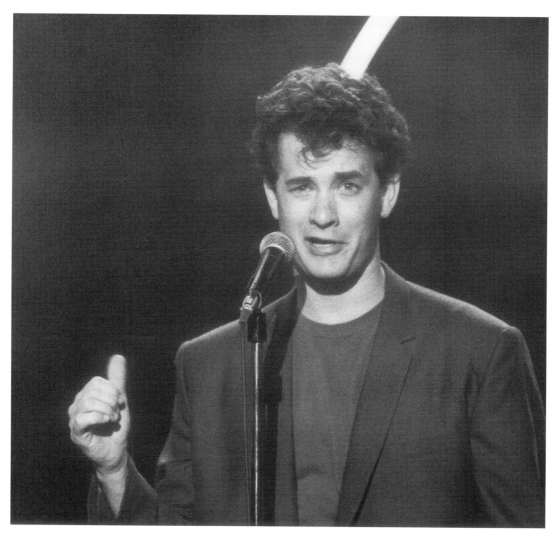

The 1987 film Punchline, *starring Tom Hanks and Sally Field, showed the difficult grind a stand-up comedian must go through to become a star. In order to become a star, Tim Allen traveled the country performing in clubs like the Punchline in Atlanta.*

has for his tools and the complex confusion men feel over women, Tim soon recognized that his humor appealed to everybody. Men went to his concerts and comedy club appearances wearing swine masks and grunted like cavemen after each joke. They shouted out when Tim bellowed one of his trademark lines, "Men are pigs!"

Women responded as well. They nodded their heads and smiled whenever Tim pointed out something familiar, as though their husbands or boyfriends had just done the same thing. Tim saw that women could laugh at men as much as men could. Tim told *Time:* "The more I started talking about it, the more I would get men to stand up and listen to my comedy. And then women would go, 'He's like that,' and it started getting couples to enjoy the show."

Because his act did not depend on comedy at the expense of females, everybody could revel in the fun. Gerri Hirshey reviewed Tim's act for *GQ.* She wrote that although other comedians used material that could be considered antifemale, Tim was "surprisingly intelligent. Affectionate. Easily housebroken."

Tim had begun to make a name for himself. Some people in the entertainment business were urging him to move to New York or Los Angeles, to be where the movers and shakers worked. Tim refused. Not only did Laura have a successful job in the Detroit area, but his family and friends lived there. They loved Michigan's climate and great outdoor environment, and he figured that if a successful musician like Bob Seger could stay near Detroit, so could he.

Some people may have questioned the wisdom of Tim's decision to stay in Michigan, but no one questioned his professionalism. He not only outworked his competitors, he outthought them. Tim knew the importance of self-promotion and understood that much of a comedian's work is done out of sight of the public. Michael Arkush wrote that each time Tim acted in a commercial for Eric Head, he sent a thank-you note, even though the two were old friends. A comedian told Arkush, "I'd go to my dad's office and xerox copies of bios and stuff and throw them in a manila envelope with a bad 8-by-10 [photograph] that my buddy shot in his basement in front of a sheet that we hung. Tim had professional 8-by-10 glossies."

According to Mark Gunther, Tim was one of the first comedians to videotape his performances. Tim would watch them over and over to see if he could improve his delivery, or spot how he held his hands or twisted his face at a particular moment. Tim would stand outside the comedy club after his performances so he could shake hands with the people who had paid to see him. He read every book he could find about comedy. Eric Head told Michael Arkush that Tim "was the single most focused guy I have ever met." Fellow comedian Tony Hayes said, "Tim was the kind of guy who, if he found a good book about comedy, would tell the other comics to read it."

Tim's reputation grew. Top comedy clubs in other parts of the country started to book him. With the help of Elaine Steffek, a manager who had connections throughout the Midwest, Tim's fame began to soar. Soon, he was on the road two or three weeks a month, opening for stars like Jay Leno in Denver or Atlantic City.

Tim did not hesitate to take a risk if he thought it would help his career. According to Michael Arkush, one night Tim appeared at the Punchline, one of Atlanta's hottest comedy clubs. Tim opened for the headline comic, and the unspoken rule of comedy at the time was that a secondary act should never outperform the top bill. After twenty minutes of riotous one-liners, Tim kept on for another fifteen minutes and turned the audience into a howling band. The angry headliner followed with no hope of getting the audience's attention.

Afterward, the club owner sat down with Tim and reminded him that what he had done was not the accepted practice. However, instead of dismissing him, the owner told Tim that he would be the headline act the next time he appeared. The owner had seen the crowd's reaction and knew that something special had happened that night. He was not going to let an unwritten rule stop a money-making act.

Tim had built a solid core of fans in various parts of the country; they were familiar with his name and his comedy. If he ever landed a television series or appeared in a movie, he could count on people recognizing his name.

Most importantly, he could see that his hard work on the comedy-club circuit was finally paying off. After years of performing in clubs all over the country, Tim was becoming one of the more popular stand-up comedians. It would only be a matter of time until his career rose to the next level: national stardom.

Appearances on several comedy specials broadcast on the cable channel Showtime led to Tim's own special, "Tim Allen: Men Are Pigs," which aired in 1990.

8

TIM'S CAREER
TAKES OFF

IN 1988, THE CABLE NETWORK Showtime, which had been show-casing the country's top comedy acts, came to Michigan to tape Detroit's best-known comedians—Tim Allen among them. Eric Head told Michael Arkush: "Other comics performed that night, but no one had the material or the charisma or the reaction that Tim had." Fellow comedian Jim McLean added, "He put everybody to shame. There was no denying that it was his night." The show was a hit, and Showtime asked Tim to appear on another comedy special, one featuring several of the nation's popular stand-up comedians.

Elaine Steffek was sending tapes of Tim's routine to different southern California nightclubs. Bob Fisher, the owner of the Ice House, a popular comedy club in Pasadena frequented by television producers and executives, saw one of the tapes and was impressed. As he told Arkush, "Out of every hundred tapes, we find maybe three people who we would consider headliners here. I think the Ice House is the hardest club for a comedian to get a booking at in the country. The only thing I remember about his tape was that it was a rare feeling that here was someone who was really good."

Tim followed in the footsteps of Bob Newhart, Lily Tomlin, David Letterman, and Garry Shandling, all of whom had appeared at the Ice House. Every night, there was a chance that someone important might catch his act and remember him when looking for new talent.

Gino Michellini, a top-rated Los Angeles radio disc jockey, had seen Tim on Showtime and loved his act. He told Arkush that everyone watching with him "was falling on the floor laughing. He was doing his tool-time routine, and he was hilarious." In early 1989 Michellini caught Tim's act at the Ice House and liked it so much he wanted to air some of his material on "The Five O'Clock Funnies," a seven-minute segment he ran during the evening rush hour.

Tim met with Michellini after his act and said he could use seven minutes from his routine. When Michellini played the material over the radio, his telephone rang off the hook. "In 24 hours the station got over 500 calls." Michellini later told a television reporter that Tim Allen's material had become the most requested act of "The Five O'Clock Funnies," even when Tim wasn't in town.

His triumph at the Ice House moved Tim closer to his dream of appearing on *The Tonight Show.* One night, James McCawley, who scouted comedians for Johnny Carson, came in to see Tim's routine. Tim had been told before he went on that McCawley would be in the audience, so he was prepared with his best material.

Unfortunately, although McCawley enjoyed the performance, he thought that Tim needed more time polishing his act before landing a spot with Carson. Tim was disappointed, but he was determined to get on the show.

Later in 1989, Tim appeared in an HBO comedy special hosted by comedian Rodney Dangerfield and performed in a concert in Anaheim, California, before 2,500 people. A *Los Angeles Times* review noted, "He had barely taken the stage when many in the audience started uttering his trade-

Tim's Showtime appearances led to increased visibility, and he found work at some of the hottest comedy clubs in the country. He also was invited by comedian Rodney Dangerfield to appear in an HBO special that Dangerfield was hosting in 1989.

mark pig snort. At this rate, it may not be long before Tim Allen becomes a household name."

Tim was one of five comics named for the Male Comedy Club Stand-Up Comic of the Year for 1989, given by the American Comedy Awards. He lost to Jeff Foxworthy, but Tim had taken another significant step.

All looked bright for the comedian, who now was earning over $50,000 a year for his nightclub appearances and television specials. The more his fame grew, however, the more he worried about his past. Would the story about his arrest and imprisonment for dealing drugs reach out from

As he developed his routines, Tim also worked on the physical aspects of his comedy, using a raised eyebrow or a well-timed grunt to elicit laughs from his audiences.

the past to haunt him? Reporter Doug Pullen of the *Kalamazoo Gazette,* who profiled the comedian during these years, sensed that Tim was hiding something. Could Tim keep his secret forever?

Another problem that bothered Tim as he became more successful was his association with Elaine Steffek. She had worked hard to get him to the top ranks in stand-up comedy, but Tim was now poised to enter a different, tougher world, run by Los Angeles power brokers. Steffek could handle small-time nightclub owners, but how would she fare against West Coast television executives and movie producers? Although he hated to sever their relationship, Tim knew that to succeed in Los Angeles, he needed an agency familiar with the territory.

In 1989, Tim hired Richard Baker and Rick Messina, two California promoters, to manage his career. Not only were they familiar with the ins and outs of the entertainment business in Los Angeles, but they were on a first-name basis with influential people and knew how to orchestrate a career move. As reporter Doug Pullen stated, "They were taking Tim through a very careful, methodical process to get him where they thought he could go. Baker was more the conceptualist, and had the TV know-how. Messina was more the day-to-day, get your fingers dirty kind of guy, like a road manager."

One of their first projects was to convince Showtime to tape Tim in his own television special. Since he had already appeared on Showtime, they figured that the network's executives would be receptive to a deal. Baker and Messina convinced Dennis Johnson, the vice president in charge of original programming, to catch Tim's act. Johnson normally goes to comedy clubs to evaluate a comic; instead of laughing at the jokes, he analyzes method and delivery, even when everyone else around him is breaking up. That night, Tim "made me laugh out loud," Johnson told Arkush. "He had really wonderful storytelling, and could create a situation that was very funny and relatable to the masses."

Johnson loved Tim's refreshing approach to real-life situations. "You could be eight years old and laugh, and you could be eighty years old and laugh. I thought that was very unique and different from most of the comics coming in at that time. I had not seen that kind of ability to tell those types of situations, based on true events, since Bill Cosby had come along."

Tim's managers closed the deal with Showtime. Here was Tim's opportunity to deliver his act to a big audience; of course, if the special bombed, it could hurt his career. For moral support, Tim wanted the special taped in Kalamazoo, where he figured the audience would be on his side. In Los Angeles, he was just another comedian trying to make it; in Kalamazoo, he was the local boy who had made good. It seemed appropriate, as well, for him to return in triumph to the scene of his greatest failure.

"Tim Allen: Men Are Pigs" was taped at the State Theater in July 1990. The special scored high ratings. Tim's friend Ken Calvert, a Detroit radio disc jockey who announced the show, told Michael Arkush, "I'd never seen a guy so nervous in my life. He was digging a trench. I think he knew that this was the one that was going to bring it all together."

Playing to a wild crowd of smiling women and grunting men wearing strap-on pig noses, Tim breezed through his routine about tool-worshiping men and the women who don't understand them. Tim was so hot that night that even when a power failure knocked out the television cameras, he ad-libbed and kept the audience laughing. When the evening was over, Calvert "got the chills. It was obvious that the mission was accomplished. It was like, 'Tim, it's been nice knowing you.'"

The year 1990 was a milestone for Tim Allen. He stood closer than ever to stardom. It was also the year in which he had his most satisfying personal accomplishment: he and Laura became the proud parents of Katherine, whom they call Kady. Not sure at first if he wanted children, one evening Tim was watching a young friend visiting with her father. Tim recalls in his autobiography, "I noticed her father looking at her with what can only be described as a sparkling gaze of pride, love, and friendship." The experience so moved him that Tim's doubts about parenthood melted away. Kady, he writes, "is so much pleasure to me that it's incredible."

Although he was not aware of it at the time, Tim was soon to become the head of another family that would also bring him a great deal of pleasure, not to mention wealth and fame. Executives from Walt Disney Studios were keeping an eye on this new comedian.

Home Improvement's *Taylor family, in their first season on television. Pictured with Tim, as TV handyman Tim Taylor, and Patricia Richardson, who plays his wife, Jill, are the Taylor children: Randy (Jonathan Taylor Thomas, bottom), Mark (Taran Smith, right), and Brad (Zachery Ty Bryan, top left). When the show premiered in 1991, it was an immediate success.*

9

"A RAW ELECTRIC WIRE"

ONE OF THE dullest parts of an entertainment executive's job is having to watch hundreds of actors and comedians perform in the hope of discovering one with any talent. Most of the time, it's a struggle just to remain awake.

In 1990, in the offices of Walt Disney's television and film operations, Jeffrey Katzenberg, who ran the department at the time, was screening videos with other studio executives. Katzenberg told *Time:* "We were sitting in the room practically snoring" until someone inserted a videotape of one of Tim Allen's Showtime pieces. They snored no more. "He set the room on fire. It was like everyone had touched a raw electric wire."

Katzenberg persuaded studio chief Michael Eisner to see Tim perform live at the Improv Comedy Club in Los Angeles. If Eisner liked Tim's act, Disney would make a deal with the comedian. Eisner loved the act and went backstage after the performance to tell Tim it was "top-to-bottom funny." He told Tim that Disney executives wanted to meet with him the following day to discuss ideas for a possible television series.

The next day, Tim and his team met with a group of Disney executives and lawyers in a large conference room. After some preliminary chitchat, Katzenberg spoke the words Tim was longing to hear: "The Walt Disney Corporation would like a marriage with Tim Allen."

Tim wanted to make sure that Disney's conception of a television role matched his own. He had struggled on the comedy-club circuit for too many years and invested too much time and effort creating his act to let it slip away from him just to land a television series.

"Well," he replied to a surprised bunch of executives, "Tim Allen would like to see the ring first."

Tim turned down Disney's first two offers, both based upon hit movies. One, *Dead Poets' Society,* had starred Robin Williams; Tim felt it would be useless to attempt to reprise a role that Williams had made his own. Tim rejected the second offer, a series based on the movie *Turner & Hootch,* because he didn't want to share the screen with a dog. Even though he was afraid his obstinacy might diminish Disney's interest in him, Tim figured this was his one chance to land a series on his own terms and was determined to give it his best shot. He told *People,* "I didn't want to sell out and do a sitcom that wasn't me just for the money."

Over the next few days, the concept for a television series gradually took shape. Disney hired writer-producer Matt Williams, who had helped create the successful *Roseanne* television show, to do the same for Tim Allen. He and Tim met for lunch, and by the time the meal was over they had created the show's basic format.

Tim felt strongly that the character he portrayed on the show should be like his stand-up character—a man obsessed by tools and confused by women. At work, he would host a cable television show that demonstrated construction projects, repairs, and tools, while at home he would try to balance the responsibilities of a wife and three young sons. Williams and his writing partner,

Michael Eisner, chairman of Walt Disney Co., decided that Tim Allen would be perfect for a starring role in a Disney television series after seeing his act at a Los Angeles comedy club.

Carmen Finestra, spotted the possibilities instantly, in part because all three came from the Midwest: Williams was from Indiana and Finestra from western Pennsylvania. Over the succeeding weeks, more details were smoothed out. Tim's character, the fumbling Tim "The Toolman" Taylor, was to be assisted on his cable show by Al Borland, whose expertise would often one-up Tim. At home, he would be assisted by Wilson, a neighbor who dispensed wisdom and advice but whose face was always to remain partially veiled.

An important component of Home Improvement, *which debuted in September 1991, is the relationship between Tim and Jill Taylor. Tim's wife on the series is played by Patricia Richardson, who was a late addition to the cast of* Home Improvement.

With all the details set, Tim and Disney signed an agreement. Tim celebrated in typical Tim Taylor fashion by purchasing an expensive chipper-shredder for his Michigan home. Tim also stopped at the Sportsman while he was in Michigan and told the store's owner, Charles Wilson III, "Something big is on, Charley. If it works, it's going to be unbelievable."

After working a few months with an acting instructor, Tim went to the Disney studios to see for the first time the set for his show, *Home Improvement.* He was surprised at all the props and various sets that had been built for one series. As a friend of Tim's reported to *Time,* Disney executives said, "'This is all for you.' Tim looked at it and said, 'Well, if this show doesn't work, can I have the wood?'"

Tim and Mark Taylor replace the engine in their lawnmower with one from a high-powered motorcycle in an early episode of Home Improvement. *In addition to showing Tim Taylor's relationship with his wife and family, the show also gives Tim Allen an opportunity to delight audiences with his comedy about tools and machinery.*

After ironing out a few wrinkles (in particular, replacing the actress who originally had been cast as Tim's wife with Patricia Richardson), *Home Improvement* was ready for its September 1991 debut. ABC was so impressed with the show's potential that it scheduled it before *Roseanne,* the top-rated series that season. Advertisers agreed with ABC and voted *Home Improvement* the new series most likely to succeed.

Tim's old friend Michael Souter came in from Michigan shortly before the premiere. According to Michael Arkush, Tim looked at his buddy and said, "You know, I'm going to be famous. You watch and see."

Fame did not come without a price. Tim had skirted the story of his drug bust ever since he began performing. Although his close friends in the business knew the details, he had never volunteered any information to anyone else. Even Disney's executives knew nothing of the affair. Tim reasoned that he had paid for his crime and the past was the past; still, he feared that a disclosure of his arrest and imprisonment would damage his career. As he became more famous, however, the possibility became more real that he would have to face the matter squarely. Some of his comedian friends even teased Tim that they would be happy to keep his secret for $50,000.

Just before the show's first episode, Tim learned that a tabloid was planning to publish the story of his drug-dealing days in Michigan and his subsequent incarceration. He was petrified. Shocked Disney executives scrambled to present the best possible front.

Tim decided that his best approach was to disclose to the American public every detail of his past. His main concern was for his family. He had embarrassed his mother and everybody else during the arrest and imprisonment, and he hated to drag them through the dirt again. But when he talked to his mother, she told him to speak out. As Tim told the *Detroit News,* "My mom and family said, 'You haven't had a lick of trouble since. What have we got to hide?'"

Wilson (played by Earl Hindman), Tim Taylor's next-door neighbor, is the show's voice of reason. Wilson, whose face is always partially hidden, gives Tim advice and insights. "He's the man that doesn't judge you, the man that makes you see the better side of you," Tim explains.

Tim next had to face the crew of his show. Patricia Richardson told a television reporter that Tim called the entire crew together to tell them about his past. "It was a torturous moment. It was very difficult to watch, and we all felt very sympathetic to him." His wife, Laura, told *People:* "It was an extremely intense couple of weeks. If we were Three Mile Island, we would have had a meltdown."

All Tim could do now was tell his story and hope the public forgave him. He told *Ladies' Home Journal,* "I trusted the American people to understand what had happened, that I'd been a stupid kid, had learned my lesson and had gotten my life on the right track."

Tim and Disney gave the story to *USA Today* so that it would appear all over the country simultaneously. The piece ran on August 16, 1991, under the headline, "Budding

Richard Karn, who plays Tim Taylor's assistant, Al Borland, often shows up his boss on the weekly series.

Star Owns Up to a Criminal Past," and not only detailed Tim's legal difficulties but included statements from his family and associates. Robert Iger, the president of ABC Entertainment, told *USA Today,* "As far as we're concerned, this is something in Tim's past that he's taken care of. It will not, in any way, diminish our enthusiasm for the

show or for Tim Allen. We don't view it as a problem and
don't think a big deal should be made out of it." And Matt
Williams stated that, far from being critical of Tim Allen,
the public should be proud of the success he carved out of
a dismal beginning: "This is about a guy who got a second
chance, and look at what he did with it."

The story evoked strong praise for Tim. His openness
and candor defused a potential time bomb, and a forgiving
nation was now ready to see what he had to offer on television. Forget the past, everyone seemed to be saying, and
get on with your future. For the first time since he was
released from prison, Tim Allen could breathe easy about
his past. The specter had been removed.

Reviews following the series debut were generally
favorable. *Rolling Stone* loved Tim as his television character, Tim Taylor, and *New York Newsday* reported that the
show was "a comedy of substance about the male spirit
and how it impacts on people and things around him."

Home Improvement was a hit with the viewers. By mid-
season it had broken the top ten, and by the summer of
1992 it was the highest-rated new show and number five
overall. *TV Guide* estimated that more than 30 million
people watched Tim Allen and company each week.

The show's popularity relied on several factors. Fans
responded to the genial family atmosphere it depicted.
Tim's character is a loving, if bumbling, spouse and father
who has a warm relationship with his wife and sons. He
always tries to do the right thing; like many men, he
inevitably goofs up. Matt Williams told *Time* that people
like Tim Allen because "I think what people see in Tim
Allen is a man-child. He's attractive, sensitive, and strong,
and he's a little, impish 12-year-old boy. You feel like he
could be you." Men like his funny remarks and outrageous
behavior, and women relate to his vulnerability and his
self-doubt.

As Tim Taylor embarks upon project after project,
destroying everything that gets in his way, his wife, Jill,

deftly handles each situation as it arises. She raises the three boys, worries about problems, and deals with Tim. They argue, but that only makes them more appealing to viewers because it makes the Taylors more like an average family.

Next door to the Taylor family is the show's voice of reason, Wilson. As Tim explained to the *Detroit Free Press,* "Wilson is every grandfather and father that has died in my life that I've missed. He's the man that doesn't judge you, the man that makes you see the better side of you." Wilson, whose face is partly hidden by the fence separating the two backyards, dispenses the insights from two of Tim Allen's favorite books: Robert Bly's *Iron John: A Book about Men,* which presents the male point of view to a world that Bly feels has been too influenced by feminism, and Deborah Tannen's *You Just Don't Understand: Women and Men in Conversation,* which asserts that men and women possess different communication skills that make it difficult for them to understand each other.

Tim Allen began to enjoy his success. On November 13, 1991, his dream came true: he appeared with Johnny Carson on *The Tonight Show.* The comic banter they exchanged moved Carson to declare his admiration for the young talent. And in what a Hollywood insider told *USA Today* was "an unprecedented achievement for such a newcomer to Hollywood," Allen cohosted the 1992 Emmy Awards ceremony. He won the 1994 People's Choice Award for best male television performer and the 1995 Golden Globe Award for best actor in a musical or comedy series.

According to Carmen Finestra, Tim's easygoing nature "has made [the *Home Improvement* set] a great place to work." Tim allows no detail to escape his attention—lighting, camera position, or his own preparation for a scene. A perfectionist, Tim makes sure that everything is done right; too many times in his life, something unexpected grabbed hold of his world and shook it horribly and violently. For Tim, quality is the norm rather than the exception.

Tim is disappointed that the show has never won an Emmy. Every year, another comedian and a different comedy series has walked away with the television industry's top prize. He told *Time:* "It hurts me because I have so many people I feel for. I get rewarded for this, but for the crew and the people who really grunt to get things done on the show—well, I take it as an affront to all of them."

In 1994, when the show had again been snubbed by the Emmys, Allen hosted his own award show for the crew in which he handed out trophies in the form of six-inch screws he called "Homeys." Although there was no one to blame that year but his own staff—his support personnel had forgotten to submit his name before the Emmy deadline—he felt that the show deserved recognition.

At least his network believed in the show's power. ABC was so impressed with *Home Improvement's* ratings that for the second season, they switched its time slot from Tuesday to Wednesday so it could go head-to-head with television's other popular comedy, *Seinfeld.* When *Home Improvement* drew higher ratings than its competition, ABC moved it back to Tuesday for its fourth season to take on another powerhouse, *Frasier.* Again, Tim's show drew higher ratings.

Not everything has been a bed of roses for Tim Allen. He can't go home without being deluged by fans or go to a store without being recognized. As he told the *Detroit Free Press,* "I'm not the same person anymore. I attract crowds where I don't want to attract crowds." He has fought hard to get where he is, and despite the drawbacks of being a celebrity, he enjoys the experience. "I'm having a great time," he asserts. "Sometimes I feel guilty, I'm having so much fun."

Tim Allen displays his four trophies after the 1995 People's Choice Awards. He was selected Favorite Male TV Performer and Favorite Actor in a Comedy Motion Picture, Home Improvement *was named Favorite Comedy Television Series, and his film* The Santa Clause *was chosen Favorite Comedy Motion Picture.*

10

"MY DREAMS ARE COMING TRUE"

THREE YEARS AFTER *Home Improvement's* debut, Tim Allen's career moved into two other areas: movies and books. Disney wanted to take advantage of his enormous popularity and have him star in a movie. After looking over several screenplays, Tim chose one about a divorced man who rebuilds his relationship with his son by substituting for Santa Claus. Tim loved the story and convinced Disney executive Jeffrey Katzenberg to let him do the movie.

Shooting for the film began in Toronto in 1994, after Tim had completed his third season for television. Between scenes, Tim worked on the other project Disney was pushing him to complete—a book. Although Disney offered him a ghostwriter, Tim wanted to write the book himself. During breaks, he headed for his trailer and wrote. *Don't Stand Too Close to a Naked Man,* published in 1994, pieces together incidents from Tim's life with his comic observations. By the end of the year, the book was first on the New York Times best-seller list.

When *The Santa Clause,* his first film, opened in November 1994, it was an instant hit at the box office. Tim had performed an entertain-

ment hat trick: His television show, his movie, and his book were all number one at the same time. Few television stars can transfer their popularity from the small screen to movies; Tim managed to accomplish not only this but had become a publishing success as well.

Tim wanted only a small measure of recognition. As he told *Time:* "It's so cheesy, but I just want a little plaque that says: No. 1 TV Show, No. 1 Book, No. 1 Movie. Just

When The Santa Clause *opened in November 1994, it quickly became a top box-office hit. At the same time,* Home Improvement *was the number-one-rated show on television, and his book* Don't Stand Too Close to a Naked Man *was atop the best-seller list.*

something for me, because I worked so hard I almost died: 18-hour days getting in and out of a fat suit, typing [my book] on my laptop. I looked forward to this day, right before Christmas, when it would all be over."

Tim's success granted him a power that surprised even him. He told *Time* that now, when he attends meetings, "if I start to say something, everybody shuts up. And any idea I say, people go, 'Oh yeah!'"

Tim hugs television spouse Patricia Richardson during an awards ceremony. Richardson told Good Housekeeping *magazine that she respects the characters of Jill and Tim Taylor because they "are in love, . . . like each other, and are best friends."*

With fame comes new responsibilities, and each takes time away from his schedule. He is deluged by the press for interviews. Although he may not want to grant them all, he understands this is part of his job. He told the *Detroit Free Press:* "Tim Dick is sick of doing interviews. Tim Allen goes, 'Hey, how are ya, how ya doin'?'"

Tim credits his prison experience for helping him handle the enormous demands made on his time. He told *USA Today*, "Had I not made that mistake and learned from it, I wouldn't have the strength or the peace of mind to do this now and not let it affect me."

His success has also made him more reflective about his father. Tim wishes his father were alive to see his son a success. "I would like to have known him now that I'm a man." He knows his father would be proud of what he has done. Still, Tim struggles with guilt over his rise to the top. He told Oprah Winfrey that everything happens for a purpose, and "I wouldn't be who I am now, and I really love who I am now, without [his death] having happened."

His success has enabled Tim to provide a comfortable lifestyle for Laura and Kady. He is very proud of his family, and takes parenting very seriously. He told *Biography Today*, "I keep thinking that she—any kid—could potentially ruin or rule the world. What a responsibility. And there's no manual." When Kady brought home her school report card recently, Tim was heartened by her teachers' comments. "They just said the sweetest things about my daughter," he wrote. "I just beamed. I got this grin on my face and looked in the mirror and said, 'You look like a dork, you're so proud of your daughter.'"

Of course, Tim Allen can't walk into an ice-cream shop or a movie theater with Kady like most fathers can with their daughters, but he still takes her on outings whenever possible. If reporters swarm around, Kady will admonish them, "I'm with my dad today, not Tim Allen." Tim will allow photographers to take pictures of him but not of his daughter; he wants to keep her out of the limelight. After he saw the movie *Ransom,* about the kidnapping of the child of a wealthy man, Tim telephoned home four times in the next few hours to make sure Kady was safe.

Tim's relationship with Laura has deepened throughout his whirlwind of Hollywood agents and million-dollar deals. She serves as a constant reminder to Tim that,

Tim Allen has used his success to help others. Here he receives a pin from a Michigan organization that provides meals and transportation to senior citizens and the physically challenged. Tim donated a van to the organization.

before fame and money, there was love and Laura. Patricia Richardson, who plays his wife on the series, told *Good Housekeeping* that she respects the characters of Tim and Jill Taylor because they "are in love, that they like each other and are best friends." She added, "I feel the same is true in Tim and Laura's marriage."

In his second book, *I'm Not Really Here,* published in 1996, Tim writes fondly of Laura: "The most profound truth I've realized after being with the same woman for almost 20 years is that the good seems to be getting better, and the bad seems to be getting less bad. I love looking at her more. I love being around her more. I trust her more."

Tim maintains three residences. One house is near his old neighborhood in Birmingham, another is a cottage on a lake in northern Michigan, next to Laura's parents, and the third is in southern California, where they live while Tim is taping *Home Improvement.* Although it was damaged in an earthquake in early 1994, they have had it rebuilt. Tim loves the house because of its amazing barbecue patio, complete with a rotisserie, two grills, a sink, and a meat locker. Nevertheless, he still calls Michigan his home and returns there frequently to recharge his batteries. Among family and old friends, he can be Tim Dick and let go of Tim Allen for awhile.

Tim's success has allowed him luxuries he could only dream of when he was a boy. He collects high-performance cars, including a Ferrari, and he races his souped-up 1993 Mustang. He told *Biography Today,* "As a kid, I used to go to auto shows and look at prototype cars and wonder what it would be like to build them. Now some of my dreams are coming true."

Fittingly enough for the man who plays Tim "The Toolman" Taylor, he boasts a large assortment of power tools and at least nine motorized pieces of equipment, including a tractor, a mulcher, and two weed-whackers. In 1995, the hammer that he designed was introduced by the Hart Tool Company. Plans are in the works for bringing out his own line of tools, with the profits to be donated to charity.

That same year, Tim had a starring role in the first full-length computer-animated film, *Toy Story.* Tim provided the voice of Buzz Lightyear, a spaceman doll that competes with Woody, a toy cowboy, for the attention of their six-year-old owner. The film, which also featured the voices of Tom Hanks (Woody), Don Rickles, Jim Varney, John Ratzenberger, and Annie Potts, earned over $200 million in 1995, making it the highest-grossing family film of the year. Over 40 film critics ranked it as one of the year's best films.

Through 1996 and 1997, *Home Improvement* continued to be a top-10 hit for ABC. Tim's second book, *I'm Not Really Here,* was published in 1996. It received good reviews and made the best-seller list. In the summer of

1997, Tim's second movie, *Jungle 2 Jungle,* was released. The film stars Tim as a New York City stockbroker who travels to the Amazon jungle to visit his former wife and meets the son that he never knew he had. When Tim agrees to take the 13-year-old boy back to New York for a visit, a hilarious culture clash ensues. Tim's third movie, *For Richer or Poorer,* a romantic comedy also starring Kirstie Alley, was released in December 1997.

Most important, Disney sold the rerun rights to *Home Improvement,* guaranteeing that Tim Allen will never have to worry about money. ABC offered Tim Allen $1.25 million per episode to return for an eighth season of *Home Improvement,* and in the future Tim would like to write a movie script about physics and how one person can change the world. Plus he will almost certainly appear in more movies.

Has success changed Tim Dick? Friend and radio disc jockey Ken Calvert does not think so. He told *People* that even if Tim lost everything, he would not be any different. "Tim said that if he ever lost it all, he'd go back and work in a sporting goods store. There are just so many things he could do with that equipment. . . . He'd never have a bad day."

To make sure he does not fail, however, Tim returns to his roots and appears in comedy clubs whenever he can. He knows this is where he found his fame, and he wants to stay sharp as a comedian. Even though he has performed in many nightclubs and has put on thousands of shows, Tim refuses to take success for granted. Not long ago, he returned to the Holly Hotel, where he appeared in 1983, when his comedy career was just beginning; the owner was surprised at Tim's behavior before his show. As he told Michael Arkush, "I thought Tim would just be able to walk up there and kind of get it out of the way. But Tim is pacing back and forth like it's his first night on stage, going over material, bouncing stuff off of me. I said, 'You could go out there right now and pick your nose for 40 minutes, and these people would love you.' He just wouldn't accept that. He was terrified of flopping. And this is Holly, Michigan, not Sunset Boulevard."

Tim Allen, the perfectionist, always making sure his act won't flop, is unable to relax with his success. He has learned the hard way that the things you love can be torn away from you in an instant. He does not want that to happen again.

CHRONOLOGY

1953	Timothy Allen Dick born June 13 in Denver, Colorado
1964	Father, Gerald, killed in an automobile accident
1966	Mother, Martha, marries William Bones
1967	Martha and family move to Birmingham, Michigan
1971	Hosts senior class "Swingout!" talent show; graduates from Birmingham Seaholm High School; attends Central Michigan University
1973	Transfers to Western Michigan University
1976	Graduates from college
1978	Arrested at Kalamazoo Airport
1979	Makes first appearance as a stand-up comedian under the name Tim Allen; sentenced to prison
1980-81	Serves sentence in Sandstone Federal Correctional Institution
1981	Released from prison after 18 months
1984	Marries Laura Deibel; creates "toolman" routine in Akron, Ohio
1988	Featured on Showtime in an all-Detroit special
1989	Material aired on Gino Michellini's "The Five O'Clock Funnies," in Los Angeles; appears in HBO comedy special; finalist for Male Comedy Club Stand-Up Comic of the Year; hires Richard Baker and Rick Messina to manage career
1990	Tapes Showtime special in Kalamazoo, Michigan; daughter, Kady, born; signs with Disney to create *Home Improvement* for television
1991	Reveals drug bust in interview with *USA Today; Home Improvement* debuts; appears on *The Tonight Show*

1992 *Home Improvement* highest-rated new television show; hosts Emmy Awards

1994 Receives People's Choice Award for best male television performer; first book, *Don't Stand Too Close to a Naked Man,* published and becomes best-seller; movie *The Santa Clause* opens; number-one rated movie, book, and television show simultaneously

1995 Receives Golden Globe Award for best actor in a musical or comedy series; *Toy Story* is released

1996 Second book, *I'm Not Really Here,* published

1997 Movies *Jungle 2 Jungle* and *For Richer or Poorer* open

FURTHER READING

Allen, Tim. *Don't Stand Too Close to a Naked Man.* New York: Hyperion, 1994.

———. *I'm Not Really Here.* New York: Hyperion, 1996.

———. "The Joy of Doing It Yourself." *Popular Mechanics,* April 1993, 68-69.

Arkush, Michael. *Tim Allen Laid Bare.* New York: Avon Books, 1995.

Gunther, Mark. "The Fall and Rise of Tim Allen: From Screwup to Superstar." *Detroit Free Press Magazine,* February 1995, 7-17.

"Real Men Laugh Last." *People,* July 1992, 105-108.

Scott, Vernon. "If I Were Married to Tim, I'd Have Done Away with Him Long Ago." *Good Housekeeping,* June 1994, 62-64.

"Tim Allen." *Biography Today,* April 1994, 9-15.

"Tim Allen." *Bon Appetit,* August 1994, 102.

Zoglin, Richard. "Tim at the Top." *Time,* 12 December 1994, 76-81.

APPENDIX

ORGANIZATIONS THAT DEAL WITH COCAINE ADDICTION OR SUBSTANCE ABUSE

COCAINE ADDICTION

Cocaine Anonymous World Service Office
PO Box 2000
Los Angeles CA 90049-8000
Phone: (310) 559-5833
Fax: (310) 559-2554

24-hour Cocaine Hotline
Provides treatment referrals and information
1-800-COCAINE

SUBSTANCE ABUSE HOTLINES

Al-Anon/Alateen Family Group
1-800-344-2666

ALCOHOL TREATMENT REFERRAL HOTLINE
1-800-ALCOHOL

Alcoholics Anonymous World Services Inc.
(212) 870-3400

Center for Substance Abuse Treatment
Referral Service
1-800-662-HELP

Marijuana Anonymous World Services
1-800-766-6779

Nar-Anon Family Groups
(310) 547-5800

Narcotics Anonymous
(818) 773-9999

**National Council on Alcoholism
and Drug Dependence Hopeline**
1-800-622-2255

Rational Recovery Systems
1-800-303-CURE

Secular Organizations for Sobriety (SOS)
(310) 821-8430

SMART Recovery Self-Help Network
(216) 292-0220

INDEX

PICTURE CREDITS

JOHN F. WUKOVITS, a teacher and writer from Trenton, Michigan, specializes in history and biography. His biographies include the World War II naval commander Admiral Clifton Sprague, as well as books on Barry Sanders, Vince Lombardi, John Stockton, Jack Nicklaus, Jesse James, Wyatt Earp, and Butch Cassidy for Chelsea House. A graduate of the University of Notre Dame, Wukovits is the father of three daughters, Amy, Julie, and Karen.

JAMES SCOTT BRADY serves on the board of trustees with the Center to Prevent Handgun Violence and is the Vice Chairman of the Brain Injury Foundation. Mr. Brady served as Assistant to the President and White House Press Secretary under President Ronald Reagan. He was severely injured in an assassination attempt on the president, but remained the White House Press Secretary until the end of the administration. Since leaving the White House, Mr. Brady has lobbied for stronger gun laws. In November 1993, President Bill Clinton signed the Brady Bill, a national law requiring a waiting period on handgun purchases and a background check on buyers.